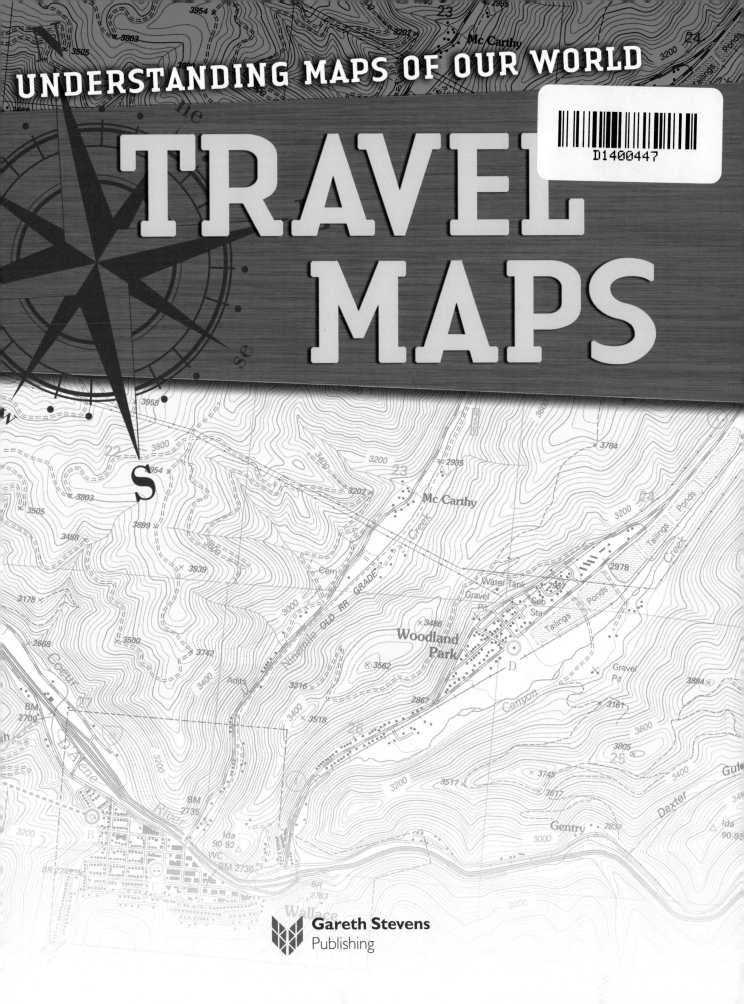

UNDERSTANDING MAPS OF OUR WORLD

TRAVEL MAPS

Gareth Stevens
Publishing

Please visit our Web site www.garethstevens.com. For a free color catalog of all our high-quality books, call toll free 1-800-542-2595 or fax 1-877-542-2596.

Library of Congress Cataloging-in-Publication Data

Hollingum, Ben.
     Travel maps / Ben Hollingum, editor.
          p. cm. -- (Understanding maps of our world)
     Includes index.
     ISBN 978-1-4339-3506-0 (library binding) -- ISBN 978-1-4339-3507-7 (pbk.)
     ISBN 978-1-4339-3508-4 (6-pack)
     1. Cartography--Juvenile literature. 2. Maps--Juvenile literature. I. Hollingum, Ben.
     GA105.6.T74 2010
     912--dc22   2009037277

Published in 2010 by
Gareth Stevens Publishing
111 East 14th Street, Suite 349
New York, NY 10003

© 2010 The Brown Reference Group Ltd.

For Gareth Stevens Publishing:
Art Direction: Haley Harasymiw
Editorial Direction: Kerri O'Donnell

For The Brown Reference Group Ltd:
Editorial Director: Lindsey Lowe
Managing Editor: Tim Cooke
Children's Publisher: Anne O'Daly
Design Manager: David Poole
Designer: Simon Morse
Production Director: Alastair Gourlay
Picture Manager: Sophie Mortimer
Picture Researcher: Clare Newman

Picture Credits:
Front Cover: Shutterstock: iofoto br; U.S. Geological Survey

Brown Reference Group: all artwork

Corbis: Michael Nicholson 35b; DigitalVision: 4m, 4b; iStock: 8, 34, 13, 17; Jupiter Images: Ablestock 5m, 38; Photos.com 7, 15, 29, 44; Stockxpert 5t, 24; Library of Congress: 32; Shutterstock: 28; Ayazad 42; Can Balcioglu 41; Thomas Bedenk; Jason Cheever 18; Vladislav Gurfinkel 4t; Oleksndr Katinichenko 30; Kwieczewski 16; Irena Tischenko 40; Evgeny Vasenev 19; Steven Wright 5b

Publisher's note to educators and parents: Our editors have carefully reviewed the Web sites that appear on p. 46 to ensure that they are suitable for students. Many Web sites change frequently, however, and we cannot guarantee that a site's future contents will continue to meet our high standards of quality and educational value. Be advised that students should be closely supervised whenever they access the Internet.

Manufactured in the United States of America
1 2 3 4 5 6 7 8 9   12 11 10

CPSIA compliance information: Batch #BRW0102GS: For further information contact Gareth Stevens, New York, New York at 1-800-542-2595.

Contents

The Changing Shape of the World

1400

This map shows the world known to Europeans in the fifteenth century: Europe and parts of Asia and Africa.

1700

1600

In this seventeenth-century map, only the interior of North America and the southern oceans remain empty.

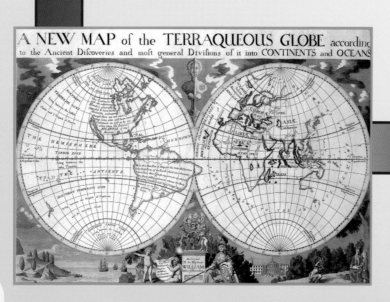

1800

This map reveals more information about Australia, but the northwest coast of North America and most of the Pacific Ocean remain unknown.

This sixteenth-century map fills in the coasts of Africa and India, the Caribbean islands, and parts of South America.

1500

In this sixteenth-century map, South America is only roughly shaped; the northwest coast of Australia has become part of the legendary "southern continent."

The first photographs of Earth from space were taken only in the 1960s.

1900

This world map was drawn in 1875, when Europeans were at the height of claiming colonies in other lands.

Introduction

This is a volume from the set Understanding Maps of Our World. This book looks at how maps and mapping help travelers find their way.

UNDERSTANDING MAPS OF OUR WORLD IS AN eight-volume set that describes the history of cartography, discusses its importance in different cultures, and explains how it is done. Cartography is the technique of compiling information for, and then drawing, maps or charts. Each volume in the set examines a particular aspect of mapping and uses numerous artworks and photographs to help the reader understand the sometimes complex themes.

After all, cartography is both a science and an art. It has existed since before words were written down and today uses the most up-to-date computer technology and imaging systems. Advances in mapmaking through history have been closely involved with wider advances in science and technology. Studying maps demands some understanding of math and at the same time an appreciation of visual creativity. Such a subject is bound to get a little complex at times!

About This Book

This book examines the different maps that have been produced over the centuries to aid travelers. One of the most important uses of maps is, of course, for traveling. Human beings have wandered across the face of the earth more than any other species. Maps are important for both long and short journeys; children grow up exploring their environment using "mental maps" of their local area, while explorers and pilgrims used maps of much larger areas to plan their journeys. Other travelers who use maps include tourists, motorists, sailors, and airplane pilots. In order to use a map effectively on your travels you need to be able to read it and interpret it correctly.

➡ **For people visiting new places, maps are very important. If you are not familiar with the landmarks, the tall buildings and enclosed spaces of a modern city can be very disorienting.**

Before Maps

Do we actually need maps? Most likely you would think they are essential, but many societies in the past and even today go through their lives without needing a map.

A GOOD EXAMPLE OF SUCH A CULTURE IS THE aboriginal people of Australia. The aborigines have their own unique view of the land and our planet. To them the Earth itself is sacred, since it was created by giant spiritual creatures in a period called the "Dreamtime."

All these giant humans and animals sprang from the earth and traveled across the empty continent of Australia, covering the land with a series of tracks. As they moved, the creatures sang the features of the world into existence. The "songlines" are the tracks taken by these creatures, crisscrossing over the landscape.

Where the creatures rested or sank back into the earth, sacred mountain ranges and hollows were created. Many songlines are very long, and they cover the areas of more than one tribe. Aborigines have been traveling them for centuries, often singing and dancing as they travel.

The aborigines can travel hundreds of miles through the bush and still know exactly where they are. The songlines are almost like roadmaps, but they are mental maps.

→ Aboriginal "songlines" are mental maps that include sacred sites such as the red rocks near Uluru, in the heart of Australia.

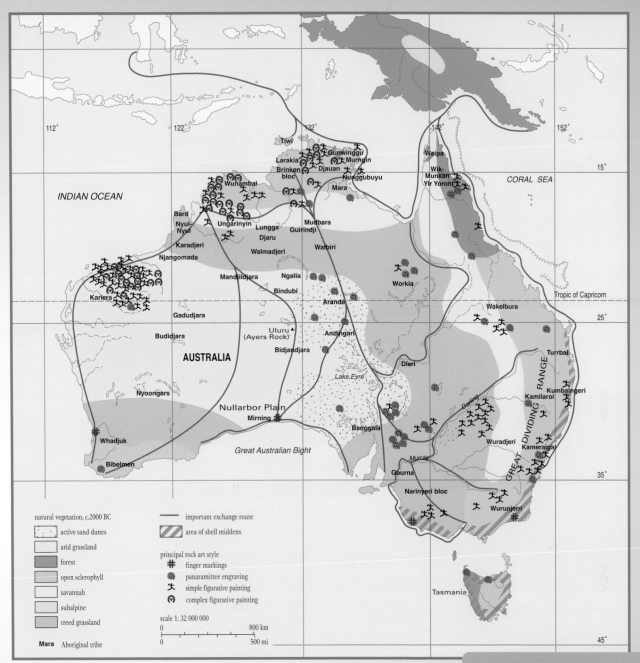

A map of the most important aboriginal sites in Australia. The whole continent is covered with songlines.

They are kept inside the mind of the person using them. If you know the correct song, you can figure out which way to walk and what you would see along the way.

Almost every creek and hill in the bush and desert has a songline associated with it. Because many of these songs are secret and considered sacred, aborigines are not pleased when others come and map the features associated with them in a scientific way. Songlines should never be mapped as a lasting record. They can be sketched out in the dust or on a piece of bark just to confirm locations, as long as the representation is later destroyed.

Pilgrim Routes

As civilizations developed, sometimes by conquering and ruling distant lands, some people needed to travel.

FOR THE ORDINARY PEOPLE, TRAVEL WAS DIFFICULT AND dangerous. One motive that was powerful enough to persuade people to take the risk was the desire to travel to sacred sites to worship.

Organized bands of such worshippers—pilgrims—date from the early days of the Christian church. Within 200 years of the death of Jesus Christ pilgrims from throughout Europe were making the journey to Jerusalem to visit its holy places.

In about A.D. 385 a nun named Egeria from northwestern Spain traveled to the Holy Land. She visited Palestine, Sinai, Egypt, Syria, and Mesopotamia (present-day Iraq). Egeria wrote a book for her sister and daughter in which she described how there were lodgings for pilgrims along the way.

About a hundred years later, in A.D. 480, the first travel guides appeared. The Bishop of Lyon, France, wrote a book about conversations with pilgrims along his route from France to Jerusalem. The information in this book was useful to travelers, describing what they might expect to see and experience, and therefore how to plan for the journey. A little later a man called Theodosius described the distances between the various sites in Jerusalem—his was perhaps the first city guidebook.

As more people got permission from the church to travel, more places to stay opened along the pilgrim routes, and more people became guides. Pilgrimage became big business. By A.D. 1000 there were so many pilgrims and so many bandits preying on them that the church tried to keep people from traveling.

From 1095 to 1291, pilgrimages were prevented by the Crusades—war waged by European Christians against the Muslim inhabitants of Jerusalem and the Holy Land.

Catholic Christendom

Orthodox Christendom
Greek rite
Slavic rite

✝ pilgrim center
— main pilgrim route, c.350–1500

0   600 km
0   400 mi

Islamic Hajj

All major religions have their sacred sites, and for Muslims a pilgrimage to Mecca—in what is now Saudi Arabia—is a duty to be perfomed at least once in a lifetime. This pilgrimage, or hajj, first became a sacred duty for the followers of the Prophet Muhammad soon after his death in 632, when traveling was perilous and exhausting. Today, millions of Muslims arrive at the holy site by airplane every year.

⬆ **Christian pilgrimage routes of medieval Europe. Those who could not afford the time and money to travel to the Holy Land visited closer holy sites.**

The Grand Tour

People can travel only if they have the leisure time and the money to do so. The first group to travel extensively for pleasure were rich young men of the eighteenth century in Britain, who made a "Grand Tour" of Europe as part of their education. The first true guidebooks with maps gradually began to appear around this time.

Early Travel Maps

Maps for travelers do not usually supply a great deal of information about the whole landscape traveled through, but concentrate instead on the route taken.

VERY EARLY MAPS WERE CARVED ON STONE AND SO WERE not portable. People probably sat around them and discussed routes, using the carvings to teach. The earliest travelers had to keep that knowledge in their heads. That was obviously very difficult for long journeys, and eventually people made maps on materials they could take with them. The Aztecs used animal skins and agave fibers, while Native North American peoples drew on birch bark.

Roman Route Maps

The Romans—who built an empire that covered most of Europe at its height in the second century A.D.—sent people long distances to trade, work, or fight. They used maps drawn on scrolls. The maps were developed from written directions that described routes. They used symbols to present the same information in a more compact form.

Strip Maps

As we have seen on pages 10–11, pilgrims in the Middle Ages were among the first land travelers. There were pilgrim hostels a day's walk apart, and most pilgrims received instructions from the hostel owner to help them on to the next stage. Pilgrim maps were eventually produced for this purpose. They show the route as a straight line, with no twists or turns but with bridges, rivers, churches, cathedrals, towns, and hostels. The main problem was that there was no scale, apart from the knowledge that hostels were about a day's walk apart.

Neither the Roman maps nor the pilgrim strip maps were particularly accurate. It was the terrible dangers of the sea that prompted the creation of the first accurate maps. Portolan charts that showed coastlines and harbors, hidden dangers, and wind directions were a vital cartographic development for the traveler.

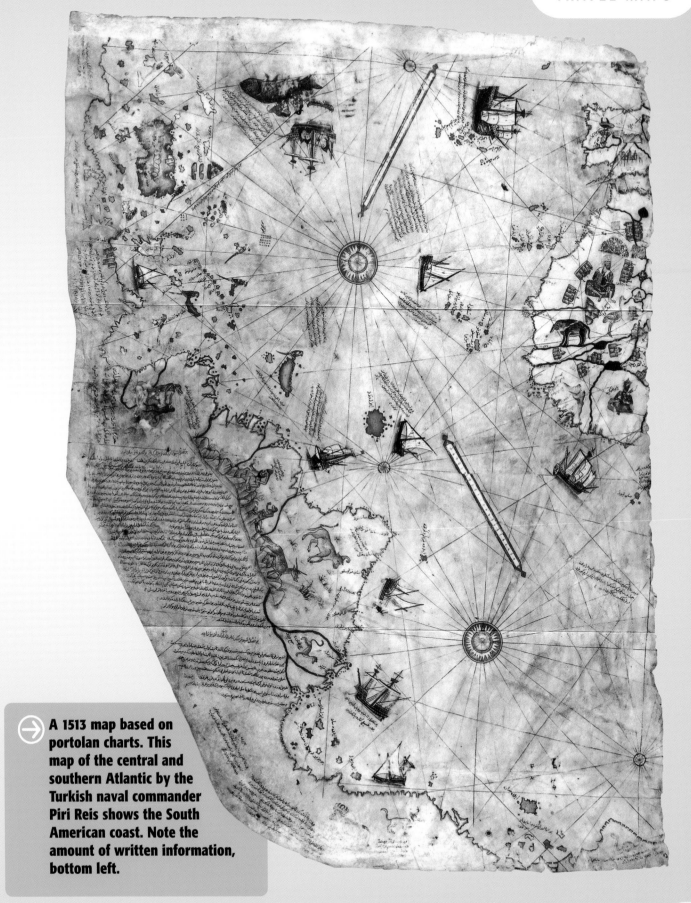

→ A 1513 map based on portolan charts. This map of the central and southern Atlantic by the Turkish naval commander Piri Reis shows the South American coast. Note the amount of written information, bottom left.

Time and Distance

Most people today travel farther than people did a century ago. They certainly travel faster, and probably a greater number of people travel now than in the past.

IF YOU ASK YOUR FRIENDS, YOU WILL find that some have traveled farther than others. Everyone travels a different distance to school because they live in different parts of town. You might expect your grandparents to have traveled only short distances when they were your age: Airplane flights were

Advances in technology have slashed the time needed to cross the Atlantic. The supersonic airliner, Concorde, could make a round trip in the time that Charles Lindbergh took to fly less than one-fifth of the route.

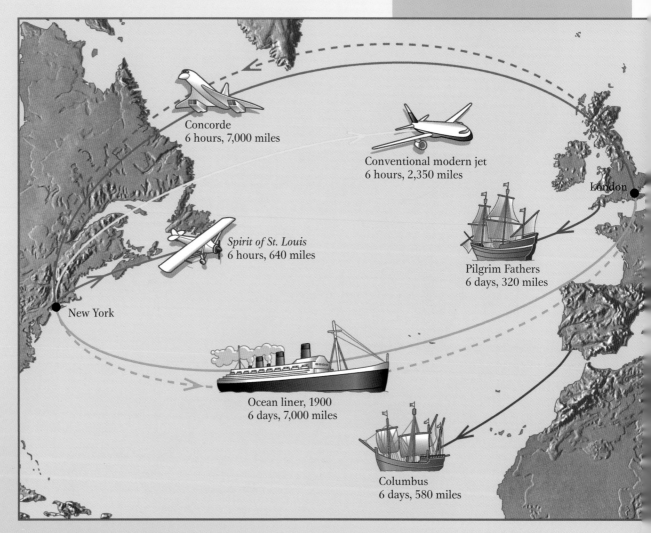

Concorde
6 hours, 7,000 miles

Conventional modern jet
6 hours, 2,350 miles

Spirit of St. Louis
6 hours, 640 miles

London

Pilgrim Fathers
6 days, 320 miles

New York

Ocean liner, 1900
6 days, 7,000 miles

Columbus
6 days, 580 miles

Imagine traveling over the vast oceans on a Viking longship. The longships are famous for their sets of oars, but it was in fact the effectiveness of the square sail that made ocean voyages possible.

expensive, cars were less reliable, and roads were not so good (although many railroads were reliable, fast, and efficient). Yet your grandfather or great-grandfather might have fought in World War II and have traveled to Europe or Asia. Your great-grandparents or great-great grandparents might have emigrated from rural areas to urban areas, from one town or city to another, or even from one country to another. On the other hand, your family could have lived in the same village for a thousand years and have rarely traveled farther than the nearest town until recently.

Crossing the Atlantic

An example of how technology has changed is the time it takes to cross the Atlantic Ocean. We do not know how long it took Leif Ericsson, a Viking, to cross the Atlantic in his small wooden boat as he did not keep a record. Columbus took 36 days to reach the Caribbean from Spain in 1492. The Pilgrims took 66 days to cross the Atlantic. By about 1900 ocean liners were crossing the Atlantic in 72 hours.

Charles Lindbergh—the first man to fly the Atlantic solo nonstop—took 33 hours in a small propeller plane in 1927. Today, an ordinary jet aircraft can cross the Atlantic in 8 or 9 hours depending on the route. Supersonic aircraft can fly across in about 3 hours.

Finding the Way

When you were young, how did you find your way around? To begin with, parents or guardians take children to places and point out notable features.

LANDMARKS HELP CHILDREN MAKE MAPS IN THEIR heads, called mental maps. There are limits to mental maps. If a young child actually draws a map, it is hardly ever to scale. Usually the boundaries and potentially dangerous features are exaggerated. The child may not know what lies beyond the neighborhood and make things up. This is something like maps made in medieval Europe, where the land beyond the boundary of the known world was shown as inhabited by monsters.

Using Landmarks

Different people find different features in the landscape interesting or memorable. When people give instructions, the landmarks they use as a guide have to be recognized by everyone. In the past, trees, hills, rivers, houses, churches, and inns have often been used to help direct people to places.

⊙➔ **This line on the wall of the Royal Observatory, England, marks the line dividing the eastern and western hemispheres. Knowing east from west is a good start for traveling!**

⬆ **Tall church steeples can often be seen from miles away, making them very convenient landmarks for travelers.**

In earlier times, before most people could read, words could not be used to identify landmarks. Inns had pictures on signs hanging above the street so that people could identify them, and they made good landmarks for travelers. Today, words are the most important landmarks in towns and cities. These include road names, numbers, and buildings that display company names.

Why Travel Maps Were First Created

Following oral instructions is difficult on a long journey. Landmarks can be missed. The person giving instructions might not have an accurate mental map of the route. A traveler needs a more reliable method of recording information to pass on to others. Even in the earliest cultures these problems existed. Members of hunter-gatherer societies who had no written language needed to communicate to each other where the wild animals or the fruit trees were. The travel map, using symbols as a sort of shorthand, was the answer.

Where Am I?

Most maps in Western cultures are drawn so that north is at the top. If you know where north is, you can then figure out which direction you are looking.

SO HOW DO YOU FIND NORTH? THE SUN RISES IN THE EAST and sets in the west. If the morning sun is on your right, then you are facing north. By scanning the landscape and looking at your map, you will be able to match landscape features to your map and get a good idea of where you are.

Rural Maps

A hill on a map is often represented by contours—lines that show all the places where the land is of equal height above sea-level. The pattern of contours on a map helps us get a general idea of the relief— steep, sloping, sweeping, and so on. But which hill is which? Some have distinctive shapes, but many do not. Some have cairns of stones or monuments. In some places there might be distinctive vegetation that matches a symbol on the map. There may also be human landmarks. There are guideposts at junctions. River bridges often have the names of the rivers on them. All of these landmarks can help travelers pinpoint their location.

➔ Cairns indicating the tops of mountains can be constructed by walkers who add a stone to a large pile. This Inuit cairn was created in the Hudson Bay area of Canada to act as a direction marker.

This walker is using a small hand-held GPS receiver to confirm her position in a relatively featureless landscape. The GPS receiver is able to indicate the direction back to her starting point, as well as her true position at any moment.

Urban Maps

Towns and cities are built on a landscape that existed before the buildings were put up. So even in a developed city, different landforms can act as landmarks—think of the distinctive switchback hills of San Francisco. In most cities there are structures that stand out, such as churches or statues that are marked on the map and can often be seen from a distance. Roads are often laid out in a grid pattern. Numbers and names make it is easy to figure out where you are by matching the road sign you see with the junction on the map.

Today, instead of directly matching the view of the landscape with the features on a map, we can precisely locate our position using modern technology. If travelers have a map and a GPS receiver, they can find out their latitude and longitude according to the receiver and match them to the lines showing latitude and longitude on the map.

Reading Maps

Map reading is not difficult if it is tackled logically step by step. The first thing to establish is orientation: Which way is north? The second thing is the scale of the map.

SCALE TELLS YOU HOW DISTANCES ON THE MAP compare with actual distances on the ground. The scale is generally represented as a ratio, or fraction. For instance, a mathematical scale of 1:63,360 is the same as writing "1 inch to the mile" (equivalent to 1.6 centimeters to the kilometer) because there are 63,360 inches in a mile.

Most maps also have the scale represented

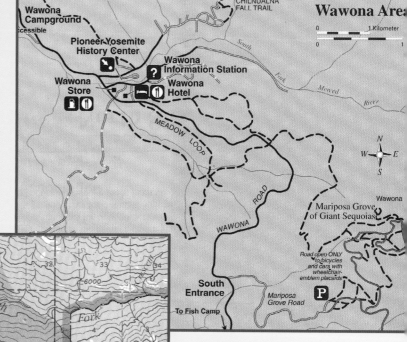

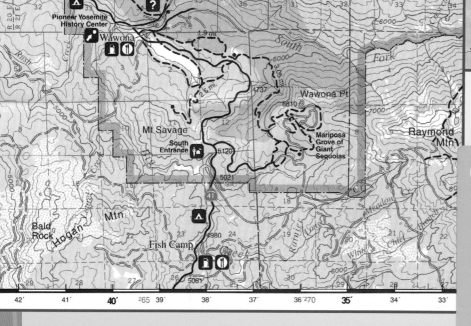

Part of Yosemite National Park, California. This is a relatively large-scale topographic map. The same printed map includes a "closeup," which is an even larger scale representation of an important tourist area (above).

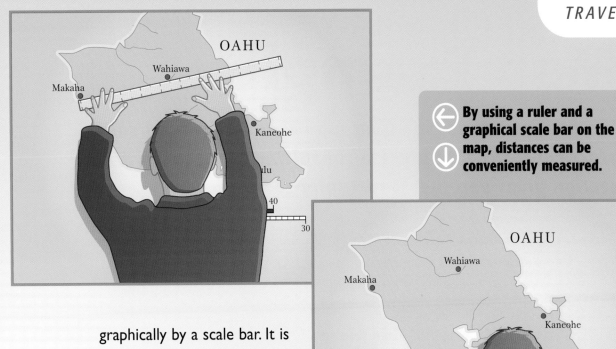

By using a ruler and a graphical scale bar on the map, distances can be conveniently measured.

graphically by a scale bar. It is a short horizontal line that for a road map is marked out in miles or kilometers (or both). Using a ruler, you can measure the distance between two places on the map and then compare that measurement with the scale bar to convert it to miles or kilometers.

Map Scales and Grids

The third term to understand when reading maps is coordinates. Latitude and longitude coordinates indicate positions of features on small-scale and some medium-scale maps. Medium- and large-scale maps often use a different system of coordinates, called a grid system.

The mapmaker marks out the map in squares by ruling a grid of horizontal and vertical lines. The squares are indicated by numbers up the sides and letters across the top and bottom. The coordinates "B3" for a location indicate that it is in the square second from the left and third up from the bottom.

The usual convention is to note the left/right measurement first and the up/down code second. An easy way to remember this is by thinking of the expression "along the hallway and up the stairs." Read along the top or bottom of the map for the correct letter, then read up one side for the correct number.

Map Example

The best way to learn about map reading is to do some practical tasks that involve consulting a real map. This section gives you the opportunity to do this.

THE MAP ON THE OPPOSITE PAGE WAS PRODUCED BY THE United States Geological Survey (USGS). It shows the small town of Wallace, Idaho. It is a topographic map because it shows information about the landscape (like rivers and woodlands), the features on the ground (including man-made features like railroads and buildings), and the shape, or relief of the ground (by using contour lines).

Positioning

The map has been surveyed on the ground and plotted from air photographs so that it is extremely accurate. The features are precisely located in relation to each other and in relation to a uniform positioning system. The positioning system is provided by the numbers around the edges of the map. These numbers measure the distance in meters away from a point that is the "origin" of the positioning system. At the origin the coordinates are 0 meters east, 0 meters north.

The position (C) of the shop in Wallace circled in red on the map is about 581,000 meters east, 5,258,000 meters north of the origin. It is at the junction of the two gridlines with these numbers. The "easting" is 581,000 and the "northing" is 5,258,000. The numbers together form a grid reference. If the position we want does not lie at the junction of two gridlines, then we must measure or estimate the grid reference. The building (D) circled in blue (toward the top right of the map), for example, has an easting directly on the 583,000 easting line. But the northing is halfway between 5,259,000 northing and the 5,260,000 northing, so the true northing for this building is about 5,259,500.

See if you can figure out the grid reference for the purple circled road junction (B). You will need to measure accurately from the nearest grid numbers to the right and above.

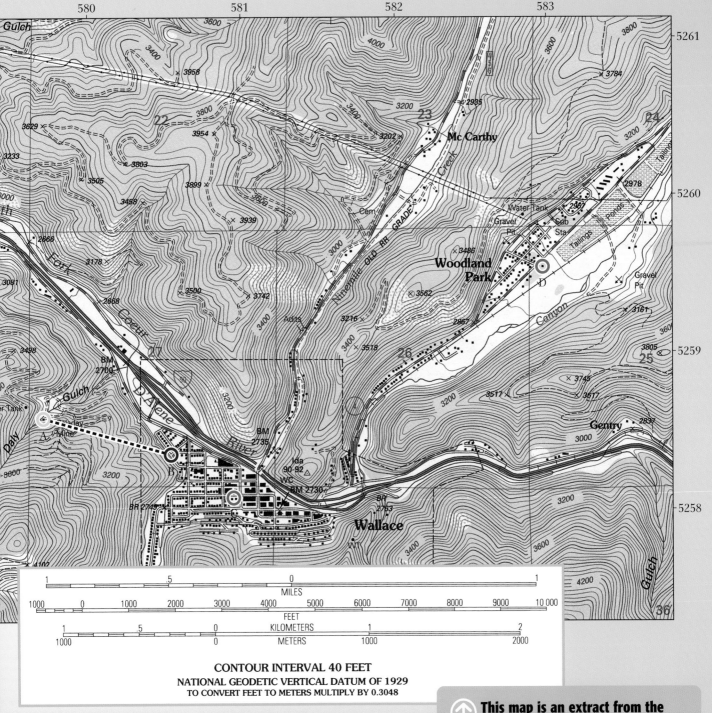

CONTOUR INTERVAL 40 FEET
NATIONAL GEODETIC VERTICAL DATUM OF 1929
TO CONVERT FEET TO METERS MULTIPLY BY 0.3048

Scale and Distance

The map has a scale of 1:24,000, so a measurement of one inch on the map is equivalent to 24,000 inches on the ground (this is 2,000 feet). Because the scale does not depend on the way in which we measure, one centimeter on the map is equivalent to 24,000 centimeters on the ground (this is 240 meters). By

This map is an extract from the official 1:24,000 USGS map. The original paper map is on the Transverse Mercator Projection and covers an area 7.5 minutes of latitude (north to south) by 7.5 minutes of longitude (east to west). It shows part of northern Idaho.

A statue commemorating the miners of the area around Wallace. On a map with a large enough scale this statue would be marked as a feature.

measuring in either inches or centimeters, you should be able to figure out the straight-line distance between the road junction B circled in purple and the building D circled in blue. You can use a ruler, then read off the distance from the scale bar underneath the map.

You cannot drive a car between the road junction and the building in a straight line. Instead, you have to plan a route, which in this case will take you through the town of Wallace and across the river by one of the bridges. You can figure out the distance along the roads and tracks chosen. That can be done by adding up the lengths of the whole series of straight-line sections that together form the route, or you can lay out a piece of thin string or cotton along the route, stretch it straight, measure it, and then figure out the distance. What is the road distance from the road junction (B) to the building (D)?

Direction

There is no north arrow on this map to show which direction north is, but the grid of numbers helps us. Horizontal lines across the map from the numbers go directly east-west, and vertical lines up and down the map from the numbers point north-south. We can draw lines like this when we want to calculate a bearing. In the real world the angle away from north that you are facing or traveling is called the bearing; and because it is an angle, it is written in degrees. When you are facing due north, your bearing is 0 degrees. If you are traveling due east, your bearing is 90 degrees; due west is 270 degrees.

It is quite easy, therefore, to use your protractor to measure the angle from north-south grid lines to the direction you are traveling. The straight line, for example, from the purple road junction to the blue building has a bearing of about 62 degrees.

Height

The heights of places above sea level are shown on this map in two ways. Over most of the map there are contour lines (or "contours") that join places of equal height. On this map the interval between the contours is 40 feet (12 m). If you were to walk up a hill and cross 7 contours on the map, you would have climbed 280 feet (85 m).

The contour lines are shown in brown and are made thicker every 200 feet (61 m). Some of them are also given numbers to help you figure out the height of every contour.

By knowing the height of the contour lines, the slopes on the ground can be visualized. From the the Caladay Mine circled in yellow (A) to the road junction (B), for example, you are going downhill. Can you estimate the height above sea level of each of these points? How far downhill are you actually going on that walk?

The heights of some important and visible places are given by printing the height above sea level alongside them. Many of the mountain tops in this area have numbers like 3954 with a cross to mark the exact summit.

Water always flows downhill, so there is a relationship between the creeks, streams, and rivers and the contour pattern. Can you figure out which way the main river on this map (the South Fork Coeur d'Alene River) is flowing? It is possible to figure it out by looking at how the contours cross the river at various locations.

Other information can be obtained by looking at the pattern of contour lines. If there are many contours close together, the ground in that area will be steep; but where there are few contours, the ground will be flat. The towns and buildings in this area, as well as the roads and railroads, tend to be on flat ground. The woodland and forest areas (colored green on this map) are mainly on the steep slopes.

How to Create a Cross-section

This is a scale drawing representing the view as it would appear from the side if a cut had been made into the surface between any two points. To make a cross-section, prepare a vertical height scale on a piece of paper as shown here. The scale should run from the lowest to the highest points between the two locations. Place the edge of the piece of paper along the line between the two locations on the map. In this case the line runs from the Caladay Mine to the road junction in Wallace. Mark on the paper where the contours cross the edge of the paper, and number every mark with its height. You might not need to mark every contour—it depends on how accurate you need to be. Draw vertical lines down to the correct height for each contour on the scale. Then join them as shown.

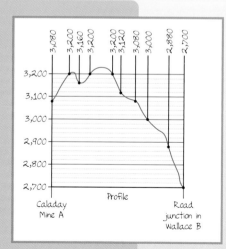

In the northern part of the map there are some straight black lines indicating electricity transmission lines, around which the forest has been felled (there is an avenue through the green area).

Cross-section

It is possible to prepare a fairly accurate sketch showing what the slopes actually look like in "cross-section." The diagram to the left shows how to create a cross-section along the line from the Caladay Mine (A) to the road junction (B), marked out by the dotted line. You can draw cross-sections between any points on the map in this way.

If cross-sections are accurate, it is possible to figure out the slope or gradient between places. The straight-line distance between the road junction and Caladay Mine is 2,820 feet (860 m), and the cross-section shows that the mine is about 380 feet (116 m) higher than the road. The average gradient is height over distance: 1/7.4.

Human Activity

Reading a map can give us clues to the local history, ecology, landscape, and agriculture of an area. The area around Wallace developed when silver mining started in 1884, and some of the mines that are still productive are indicated on the map. The tracks of some disused railroads are marked "Old RR Grade."

Map Symbols

This map has very few symbols representing important features. "BM" means bench mark, an accurate height point; WT means water tank. On some USGS maps, where there is a lot of information to fit into a small space, many more symbols and abbreviations are used.

VEGETATION	
Woods	
Scrub	
Orchard	
Vineyard	
Mangrove	
GLACIERS AND PERMANENT SNOWFIELDS	
Contours and limits	
Form lines	
ROADS AND RELATED FEATURES Roads on Provisional edition maps are not classified as primary, secondary or light duty. They are all symbolized as light duty roads.	
Primary highway	
Secondary highway	
Light duty road	
Unimproved road	
Trail	
Dual highway	
Dual highway with median strip	
Road under construction	uc
Underpass; overpass	
Bridge	
Drawbridge	
Tunnel	

This is an extract from the legend for USGS topographic maps. It helps the map reader understand the meaning of the symbols used. The symbols include glaciers for Alaskan mapping.

Orienteering

Orienteering is an outdoor sport that depends on map-reading and direction-finding skills. Competitors run or jog between points that have to be visited in a set order.

ORIENTEERING MAPS CONCENTRATE ON GIVING THE competitors the information they need to select a sensible route between the marked points. The maps are commonly at a scale of 1:15,000, which shows landscape features in detail. To get between these places, an orienteer must be able to read a map and to navigate using a compass. The competitor has to use the map to select routes. It may be that a direct route has obstacles, such as streams or marshes, woods and hills. A longer route could be quicker. The competitor who travels the route fastest, checking in at each "control point," is the winner.

How Does a Compass Work?

The Earth acts as if it has a huge magnet along its axis. A point near the North Pole attracts a magnetized needle in that direction. A compass has such a needle, pivoted or suspended in liquid, that always points to north. Although the magnetic poles do not quite match up with the geographic poles, for most people the two are near enough.

A compass used for orienteering. Using this type of compass, with its movable baseplate, makes navigation easier.

Orienteering competitors consider the best route through the forest—not necessarily the most direct.

The Thumb Compass

Orienteers commonly use a thumb compass. The needle has a red end pointing to north, and it swings freely in liquid to allow the needle to constantly realign itself. There is also a direction of travel arrow. The thumb compass has a strap that attaches to the left thumb. The right hand is left free to hold a map, and the compass is therefore more easily and quickly lined up with the map.

Using a Compass

The first principle is to know exactly where you are all the time! You can then decide how to get to the next control point by the most effective—the fastest—route. Draw a line along the route between where you are now and where you want to be on your map. Place your compass on the map so that the direction of travel arrow is pointing along that line. Keeping the compass base still, turn the turntable that holds the compass needle so that the arrow lines up with the north lines on your map. Take the compass off the map, and hold it in front of you with the direction of travel arrow pointing ahead. Turn slowly until the compass needle lines up with the north mark. Proceed in the direction of the travel arrow. Pick out a landmark in the direction of travel, and head toward it. When you reach a landmark, you can start the process all over again and eventually arrive at the control point.

Away from Land

What happens to a ship out at sea or a high-flying airplane where there are no landmarks? Can maps be used to help them travel successfully?

NAVIGATORS USE MAPS CALLED charts for finding out where they are and for plotting a course to their destination. Even though landmarks may not be visible, the charts show radio navigation aids, depth of the sea, and latitude and longitude.

Sailors have used navigational charts for centuries. Using charts is an important part of the training of mariners. This has not changed, despite the ease with which GPS can locate a ship. The mariner must still interpret underwater danger indicated by charts.

Nautical Charts

For most large ships it is mandatory to have on board the nautical chart of the sea area in which they are sailing. For ships and boats that are within sight of land, an inshore nautical chart can be used. It includes the coastline and may show landmarks such as lighthouses and prominent buildings. It also plots the positions of buoys, small islands, and hazards such as wrecks, reefs, and rocks that are a danger at low tide.

Water depths are indicated in much the same way as hills are on land maps. Lines similar to contour lines join points of equal depth, often measured in fathoms (1 fathom equals 6 feet or 1.8 meters).

The information for plotting water depths on the charts comes from measurements called soundings, usually made using sonar (echo-sounding). Visible features such as the coastline are taken from existing land maps.

Many inshore charts also show the location of navigational beacons. They may transmit radio signals or produce flashing lights at night. The number and duration of the flashes are different for each beacon, and the pattern of signals is shown on the chart. Ships can then identify each beacon in turn to figure out their position.

Aeronautical Charts

Pilots of low-flying aircraft flying over land can use ordinary topographic maps, although special maps that emphasize things that can be seen from the air are more useful. Called VFR charts (VFR stands for visual flight rules), they show prominent landmarks such as railroad tracks, highways, rivers, bridges, towns, and, of course, the locations of airports and landing strips. They also indicate the heights of hazardous obstructions such as radio towers and high hills.

Navigators of high-flying aircraft use IFR charts, where IFR stands for instrument flight rules. Such planes have to rely on instruments because useful ground features are not visible from a great height—commercial jets commonly fly at up to 35,000 feet (nearly 11,000 m). The chief navigational instrument is a radio receiver tuned to the very-high-frequency signals transmitted by a worldwide network of radio beacons. The positions of the beacons are shown on the IFR charts, and each transmits a unique signal by which it can be identified.

Small-scale Maps

Small-scale maps, which do not include much detail, are good for planning long-distance travel. They include road atlases, bus maps, and airline maps.

TO PLAN A TRIP ACROSS THE U.S., A TRAVELER MIGHT buy a road atlas, which is a collection of maps that between them cover the whole country. The first map in the atlas is a locator map, which gives three main pieces of information: the major place names, the interstate highways and their numbers, and a grid to indicate the page numbers where more detailed maps of the states can be found.

Sparsely Populated Areas

Individual state maps farther on in the atlas zoom in with more detail than the locator map. Where states are sparsely populated, a scale of 30 miles to the inch (about 20 kilometers to the centimeter) is appropriate to give the long-distance traveler a broad idea of the landscape. Prominent landmarks such as mountain peaks, lakes, forests, or airports reassure the traveler that he or she is going in the right direction.

Hazards are also marked, such as marshes and military firing ranges. There is distance information between intersections or

A stagecoach passes through the American west in the 1880s. Travel then was tough, and most passengers, very few of whom would have ever even seen a map, had little idea of where they were.

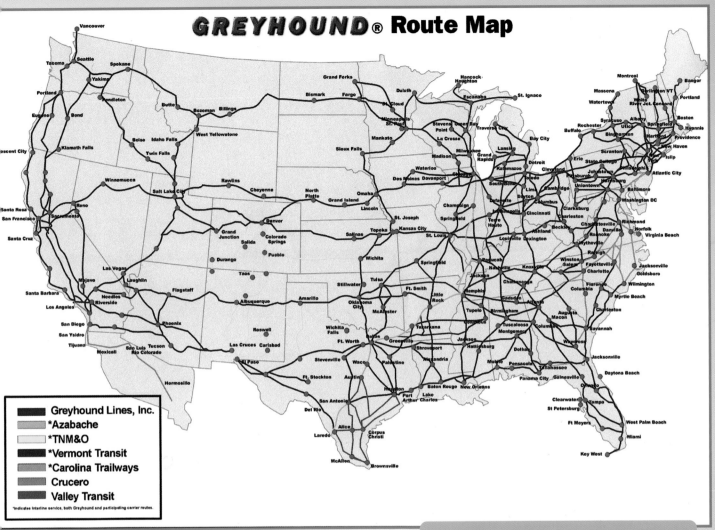

GREYHOUND® Route Map

Legend:
- Greyhound Lines, Inc.
- *Azabache
- *TNM&O
- *Vermont Transit
- *Carolina Trailways
- Crucero
- Valley Transit

*Indicates interline service, both Greyhound and participating carrier routes.

junctions, and a table above the map gives distances between the main towns and cities so that drivers can plan stops and overnight stays. Scenic areas are marked, as well as viewpoints, campsites, and picnic stops. Even with these details, however, the map seems bare.

⬆ **Today, long-distance passengers receive some simplified information about their route. The Greyhound Bus Company produces advertising material showing their extensive route network.**

Densely Populated Areas

Where many places are close together, the same landmarks are used, but the scale is increased to 15 miles to the inch (10 kilometers to the centimeter). Despite having twice the space because the scale is bigger, the map is crowded. This highlights the mapmaker's dilemma. He or she must not put in so much detail that the traveler is confused. However, he or she must give the travelers the detail needed to reassure them that they are going in the right direction.

On the Road

Road atlases cover different sizes of area. Some are of whole nations, some of regions, and some—commonly known as the A-Z type—are road maps of towns and cities.

ROAD MAPS WERE FIRST MADE POPULAR BY THE English mapmaker John Ogilby (see box opposite). The problem for him and all mapmakers was how to select for reproduction the parts of the landscape that the traveler needs for the map to be a useful tool. Ogilby succeeded because he gave enough natural landscape to help people identify landmarks, while adding just the roads, inns, and other landmarks they needed to reassure themselves that they were traveling in the right direction.

Road Atlases

The maps in a road atlas classify roads to help people through the landscape. They are divided into toll and free access. Main highways are indicated, and so are scenic routes and unpaved roads.

Maps and atlases produced for drivers are often quite simplifed. They record the most useful routes and present them in a simplified form so that users are able to read the information they require easily in the car—but not when they are actually driving!

34

Today, detailed road maps are available in the form of digital maps produced on in-car systems. Often such systems are connected to a GPS receiver or to a radio that receives up-to-date traffic news with information on delays, weather conditions, and detours.

John Ogilby 1600–1676

Ogilby was an English pioneer of road surveys and road mapping. But he had a varied career. Originally he was a dancing master and a successful theater owner in Ireland–he built a theater in Dublin. With the outbreak of the Civil War in England Ogilby was financially ruined, and he returned to England. He learned Greek and Latin, which enabled him to translate the works of the ancient poets Homer and Virgil. After the Great Fire of London in 1666 Ogilby was asked to survey some of the disputed areas of London property. As a result he set up as a printer and began to draw and sell maps. He surveyed the roads of England using an odometer, and in 1675 he published the first accurate road maps of England as a series of strip maps. *Britannia–A Geographical and Historical Description of the Principal Roads Thereof* was part of a planned world atlas and the first truly accurate road atlas in history.

Distances between intersections allow travelers to figure out how long their trip will take. Gradient is shown outside cities by contours, layer tinting, or hill shading.

The Web and GPS

By supplying a zip code to a road mapping website, today's driver can get a regional map with all junctions marked. Route plans can be accessed. Even better, GPS receivers can interact with the web not only to plan journeys but to find out how far the driver has already traveled from a stated location and how fast. In Europe some cars have CD or DVD players linked to a GPS receiver. The driver keys in a destination, and the on-board computer uses information on the CD and from the GPS to work out the route and supply a map.

Animal Navigators

For centuries people have wondered at the ability of many birds, mammals, and insects to migrate great distances.

GREEN TURTLES MAKE A 2,800-MILE (4,500-KM) ROUND trip between Ascension Island, where they breed, and their main feeding grounds in Brazil. Every autumn at least 10 million monarch butterflies migrate from southern Canada and the eastern United States to spend the winter at eleven sites in central Mexico. Some travel over 2,980 miles (4,800 km). They return each year to the same clump of trees, yet the generation that makes the return journey is not the same one that left Mexico the previous autumn. How do these animals find their way?

Sights, Sounds, and Smells

The simplest kind of direction finding is piloting. Humans use it every day. It involves local signals. Migrating geese, shorebirds, and gray whales follow coastlines, while inland migrants such as geese or caribou follow mountain ranges or large rivers. Salmon migrating across the oceans use smell—the faint scent of the rivers in which they hatched. Winds blowing over mountain ranges and waves crashing onto coasts produce low frequency sound—infrasound. Homing pigeons have been shown to use such sounds as landmarks. Their homing accuracy can be disrupted by the sonic boom of supersonic jets! Whales and other marine migrating mammals also use infrasound.

Two migratory birds of prey; Swainson's hawk (left) and the red-footed falcon (opposite, top).

The routes of two of the longest migrations by birds of prey are shown here. Eastern red-footed falcons fly from Siberia to southern Africa. Swainson's hawks fly from Alaska to Argentina. It is obvious from the map that both birds fly overland where possible, either to take advantage of thermals or to use landmarks.

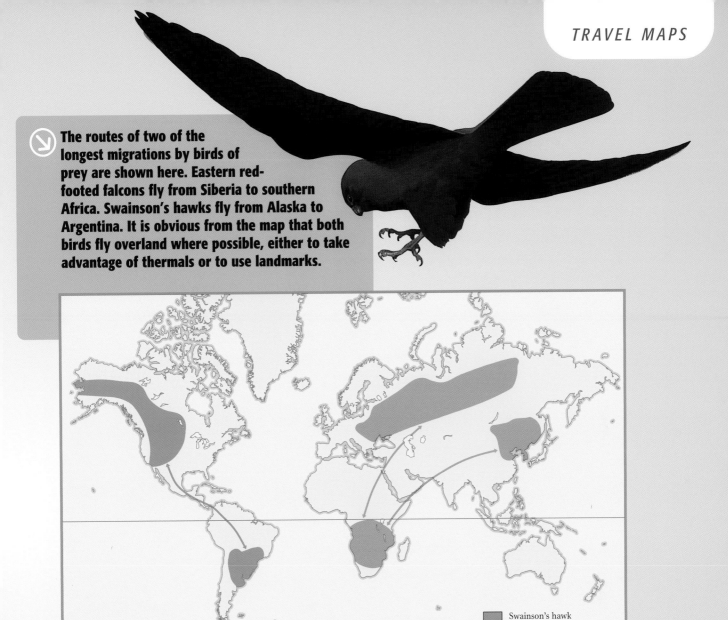

Swainson's hawk
Eastern red-footed falcon

Celestial Signs

Where there are no reliable landmarks, animals must use some kind of compass to find direction. The most obvious directional cues are the sun and the stars. The sun rises in the east and sets in the west, and moves 15° per hour. For this to be a guide the animal must have an accurate sense of time.

Most animals have a built-in biological clock that tells them whether it is morning or evening and regulates their activity accordingly. If racing pigeons are conditioned to be six hours ahead of local time and released miles from home, they fly in the wrong direction. That is because the bird thinks it is afternoon, when in fact it is midday. It therefore incorrectly interprets the position of the sun. This shows that the pigeons are using the sun and time for navigation—they do not have a mental map.

The stars, too, move across the sky with time. Experiments have shown that many birds recognize constellations and navigate by them. At the center of rotation of the stars there is a fixed point, and experiments suggest that migrating birds may use it.

Honeybees can measure distance. They seem to know the time they have spent traveling and can even compensate for wind speed and direction. Another cue is the angle of dip of the Earth's magnetic force lines, which is steeper toward the poles, and conveys north-south information. The sun and stars are risky cues, since they are often obscured. However, honeybees can detect ultraviolet light, which penetrates clouds.

Preprogrammed for Travel

Many animals and birds need to change direction during their migration. For example, birds moving south from northern Europe often change direction at the Mediterranean Sea to avoid flying over the Sahara Desert. The birds use a combination of distance, flying time, and direction to orient themselves. They travel in one direction for a certain distance or time, then change to another direction. This sense is programmed into the birds from birth.

 A newt basks on a rock. The most impressive thing is not the remarkable appearance, but the newt's ability to use magnetism for navigation.

The Dancing Compass

Honeybee workers forage for nectar to bring back to the hive to feed the colony. When a bee finds a good source of nectar, she returns to the hive to recruit more foragers. But how does the bee signal where the new food source is in the darkness of the hive? The returning bee performs a dance on the vertical comb in the hive. If the food is close to the hive, the bee performs a figure-eight "waggle dance." The bee waggles her abdomen from side to side during the straight part of the dance. The direction in which the dancer faces during her dance points to the food site in relation to the sun. The speed of the dance relates to the distance between the hive and the feeding sites. The closer the food, the faster the dance. During the dance the whirring of the dancing bee's wings is detected by the bees surrounding her. Honeybees' hearing organs, located in the joints of their antennae (feelers), are closely tuned to the frequency of these sounds. From time to time the listening bees squeak by pressing their bodies against the comb. This vibrates the comb, causing the dancer to stop and give out samples of the food for the new recruits to learn the smell and taste of it. If the food source is closer to the hive than about 250 feet (75 m), the bee performs a simpler dance with no waggle—the "round" dance. The waggle dance is shown on the left above; the round dance is on the right.

Magnetic and Electrical Maps

Newts seem to use the "background" magnetic field of the whole Earth or small, local changes in magnetic inclination over distances of just a mile or so to navigate. This gives a latitude coordinate. Together with one of the other cues mentioned—the sun's position, landscape features, and so on—this can become a two-coordinate map. Although newts would normally not range much more than a mile from their home, when transported about 30 miles (50 km) away, they can find their way home.

Some fish generate electricity, creating an electrical field around themselves. Objects moving in the water nearby deflect the field. The size of the deflection depends on the size and nearness of the object. Not only does this warn of danger, but it may also provide the fish with an electrical map.

Glossary

Words in *italics* have their own entries in the glossary.

aborigines – the original inhabitants of an area, in particular the original inhabitants of Australia and their descendants

aeronautical – relating to aircraft or aircraft flight

agave – a tall plant with thick fleshy leaves, native to tropical America; its fibers were used by some ancient American peoples as a crude form of paper

altitude – height or vertical distance above mean sea level; or the degrees of elevation of a star, the sun, or the moon above the horizon

Aztecs – a people who in the 15th and early 16th century ruled a large empire in what is now central and southern Mexico; they probably came from the northern Mexican Plateau in the 12th century

bearing – the direction someone is heading measured as an angle away from north; due north has a bearing of 0 degrees, while due west has a bearing of 270 degrees. Bearing is also sometimes used to describe angular position or direction in relation to any two known points.

cairn – a pile of stones set on a hill or mountain to mark a spot for travelers, or as a memorial to someone who died nearby

cartography – the skill of making maps; somebody who collects information and produces maps is called a cartographer

compass – an instrument showing the direction of *magnetic north* using a magnetic needle; *bearing* can be calculated by using a compass

contour – an imaginary line connecting places in the landscape that are at equal height above (or below) sea level. The distance of contour lines from each other on a map shows how steeply or gradually land rises.

coordinates – the pair of values that define a position on a graph or on a map with a coordinate system (such as *latitude* and *longitude*). On a map the coordinates "55°N 45°E" indicate a position of 55 degrees north of *latitude*, 45 degrees east of *longitude*

cross-section – a scale drawing that represents the view of a landscapeas it would appear from theside, formed by a plane cutting into the surface between any two points

The magnetic compass was first used for navigation in China around 1,000 years ago. It is still an important navigational tool although it is rarely used for long-distance navigation anymore.

Cultural overlay **can make it very difficult to identify the natural shape of the land. Take this picture of San Francisco, for example—the buildings conceal the shape of the landscape they are built on.**

cultural overlay – the things that people have built over the shape of the natural landscape: things like towns, cities, roads, and reservoirs

densely populated – a large number of people living in a small area; Bangladesh is a densely populated country, with 2,000 people for every square mile, 980 people for every square kilometer. In comparison, Canada has just 8 people per square mile, or 3.5 people per square kilometer.

ecology – the study of the relationships and interactions between living things and their natural environment

Egeria – Spanish noblewoman of the 6th–7th century. She traveled to the Holy Land to visit its churches and holy places, and wrote a guidebook about them for other pilgrims to use.

emigrate – to move from one country to another and live there permanently

Ericsson, Leif – 11th-century *Viking* explorer who is thought to have been the first European to set foot on North American soil, probably in Newfoundland

generation – the period of time between the birth of your parent and your own birth, often taken to be 25–30 years for making calculations about changes in a population

Global Positioning System (GPS) – a system of 24 man-made satellites orbiting Earth and sending out highly accurate radio signals indicating where they are; a GPS receiver held by someone on Earth can interpret the signals and calculate the receiver's position

gradient – the ratio between the height difference (up or down) over a given distance and the distance traveled horizontally; it describes the steepness of a slope

Greyhound – a long-distance bus company with a network of routes throughout the U.S. and Canada

grid system – uses a mesh of horizontal and vertical lines over the face of a map to pinpoint the position of places. The mesh of lines often helps show distance of locations east and north from a set position. The *zero position* can be any convenient location and is often the bottom-left corner of the map.

hajj – the pilgrimage to Mecca expected of all Moslems, or followers of the religion of Islam (if they can afford it) at least once. The prophet Mohammad had seen himself in a dream performing the annual pilgrimage and had led his followers to Mecca in accordance with Islamic belief shortly before his death in 632.

horizontal – parallel to the horizon; in an east-west direction

One of the massive tent cities that are constructed on the outskirts of Mecca every year to accomodate the millions of Muslim pilgrims from around the world who arrive to perform the hajj every year.

hunter-gatherers – people who lived by hunting wild animals and gathering food from native plants, rather than subsisting by settled agriculture

junction – the location where two or more roads meet; an intersection

large-scale map – a map that shows a small area with a lot of detail; like a bird's-eye-view from a low height above Earth

latitude – a line that joins places of equal angular distance from the center of Earth in a north-south direction. The *equator* is at 0 degrees latitude, the *poles* at 90 degrees latitude north and south.

layer tinting – showing the *altitude* of mountains and hills on a map using bands of color to define zones where the land is between two height measurements (between 100 and 250 meters above sea level, for example)

legend – a list of all the *symbols* used on a map with an explanation of their meaning

longitude – a line connecting places of equal angular distance from the center of Earth, measured in degrees east or west of the *Prime Meridian*, which is at 0 degrees longitude

magnetic north – the northerly direction in Earth's magnetic field, indicated by the direction in which a *compass* needle points

medieval – the historical period in Europe between 500 and 1500 A.D.

migrate – to move from one place to another, but not necessarily forever. Some birds and animals migrate annually, dividing their seasons between two or more areas, as do some peoples, including *hunter-gatherers*.

nautical – relating to ships, sailors, and travel on a body of water

navigation – plotting a route and directing a ship, airplane, or other vehicle from one place to another; we now use the word to apply to journeys on foot as well

odometer – a device for recording distance on land, particularly along roads. A wheel with a known circumference rotates across the ground, and distance

is calculated by counting the number of revolutions between locations and multiplying by the circumference.

orientate – to position a map or surveying instrument, or a person, with reference to known features or to the points of the *compass*. The word comes from the Latin *oriens*, which means "rising" and refers to the sun, which rises in the east. So "the Orient" came to mean countries east of the Mediterranean.

orienteering – an outdoor sport that requires map-reading and direction-finding skills

poles – the points at either end of Earth's axis of rotation where it meets Earth's surface; the Geographic North and South Poles

portolan charts – navigational charts used by European sailors from about 1300 to 1600

Prime Meridian – the line of *longitude* at 0 degrees; by international agreement it is the line that passes through Greenwich, London, England

relief – the shape of Earth's surface, its hills, mountains, and depressions

Reis, Piri (1465–1554) – a pirate at age 12, Reis rose to become admiral of the Turkish fleet of Egypt and India. Making use of information acquired from a Portuguese prisoner who had served in Columbus's crew, Reis created a map of the known world. His map was rediscovered only in 1929.

rural – describes areas with few buildings and people

In the middle ages the Vikings, who came from Scandinavia, used their skill as navigators and shipbuilders to travel to lands as distant as Turkey, Iceland, and even North America. They used their knowledge of the sun's movements throughout the year to orient themselves.

scale – the ratio of the size of a map to the area of the real world that it represents

small-scale map – a map that shows a large area with only a little detail; like a bird's-eye-view from far above Earth

sonar – a device for detecting and locating objects underwater or measuring depth by timing the reflection of sound waves from the sea floor

symbol – a diagram, icon, letter, or character used on a map to represent a specific characteristic or feature

thumb compass – a compass with a strap that attaches to the thumb. This allows orienteering competitors to hold a map and check the compass at the same time.

topographical map – a map that shows natural features such as hills, rivers, and forests, and man-made features such as roads and buildings

urban – describes built-up areas such as towns and cities

vertical – perpendicular to the horizon; in a north-south direction

Vikings – warrior seamen and traders from Scandinavia who were prominent from the 8th to the 11th centuries

zero point or position – the point that defines the position of all other reference points on a map

Further Reading and Web Sites

Aczel, Amir D. *The Riddle of the Compass: The Invention That Changed the World*. New York: Harcourt, 2001.

Arnold, Caroline. *The Geography Book: Activities for Exploring, Mapping, and Enjoying Your World*. New York: Wiley, 2002.

Barber, Peter, and April Carlucci, eds. *The Lie of the Land*. London: British Library Publications, 2001.

Brown, Carron, ed. *The Best-Ever Book of Exploration*. New York: Kingfisher Books, 2002.

Davis, Graham. *Make Your Own Maps*. New York: Sterling, 2008.

Deboo, Ana. *Mapping the Seas and Skies*. Chicago: Heinemann-Raintree, 2007.

Dickinson, Rachel. *Tools of Navigation: A Kid's Guide to the History & Science of Finding Your Way*. White River Junction, VT: Nomad Press, 2005.

Doak, Robin S. *Christopher Columbus: Explorer of the New World*. Minneapolis, MN: Compass Point Books, 2005.

Ehrenberg, Ralph E. *Mapping the World: An Illustrated History of Cartography*. Washington, D.C.: National Geographic, 2005.

Field, Paula, ed. *The Kingfisher Student Atlas of North America*. Boston: Kingfisher, 2005.

Ganeri, Anita, and Andrea Mills. *Atlas of Exploration*. New York: DK Publishing, 2008.

Graham, Alma, ed. *Discovering Maps*. Maplewood, NJ: Hammond World Atlas Corporation, 2004.

Harvey, Miles. *The Island of Lost Maps: A True Story of Cartographic Crime*. New York: Random House, 2000.

Harwood, Jeremy. *To the Ends of the Earth: 100 Maps That Changed the World*. Newton Abbot, United Kingdom: David and Charles, 2006.

Haywood, John. *Atlas of World History*. New York: Barnes and Noble, 1997.

Hazen, Walter A. *Everyday Life: Exploration & Discovery*. Tuscon, AZ: Good Year Books, 2005.

Henzel, Cynthia Kennedy. *Mapping History*. Edina, MN: Abdo Publishing, 2008.

Jacobs, Frank. *Strange Maps: An Atlas of Cartographic Curiosities*. New York: Viking Studio, 2009.

Keay, John. *The Great Arc: The Dramatic Tale of How India Was Mapped and Everest Was Named*. New York: HarperCollins, 2000.

Levy, Janey. *Mapping America's Westward Expansion: Applying Geographic Tools And Interpreting Maps*. New York: Rosen Publishing, 2005.

Levy, Janey. *The Silk Road: Using a Map Scale to Measure Distances*. New York: PowerKids Press, 2005.

McDonnell, Mark D. *Maps on File*. New York: Facts on File, 2007.

McNeese, Tim. *Christopher Columbus and the Discovery of the Americas*. Philadelphia: Chelsea House, 2006.

Mitchell, Robert, and Donald Prickel. *Contemporary's Number Power: Graphs, Tables, Schedules, and Maps*. Lincolnwood, IL: Contemporary Books, 2000.

Oleksy, Walter G. *Mapping the Seas*. New York: Franklin Watts, 2003.

Oleksy, Walter G. *Mapping the Skies*. New York: Franklin Watts, 2003.

Resnick, Abraham. *Maps Tell Stories Too: Geographic Connections to American History*. Bloomington, IN: IUniverse, 2002.

Rirdan, Daniel. *Wide Ranging World Map*. Phoenix, AZ: Exploration, 2002.

Ross, Val. *The Road to There: Mapmakers and Their Stories*. Toronto, Canada: Tundra Books, 2009.

Rumsey, David, and Edith M. Punt. *Cartographica Extraordinaire: The Historical Map Transformed.* Redlands, CA: Esri Press, 2004.

Short, Charles Rennie. *The World through Maps.* Buffalo, NY: Firefly Books, 2003.

Smith, A. G. *Where Am I? The Story of Maps and Navigation.* Toronto, Canada: Fitzhenry and Whiteside, 2001.

Taylor, Barbara. *Looking at Maps.* North Mankato, MN: Franklin Watts, 2007.

Taylor, Barbara. *Maps and Mapping.* New York: Kingfisher, 2002.

Virga, Vincent. *Cartographia: Mapping Civilizations.* London: Little, Brown and Company, 2007.

Wilkinson, Philip. *The World of Exploration.* New York: Kingfisher, 2006.

Wilson, Patrick. *Navigation and Signalling.* Broomall, PA: Mason Crest Publishers, 2002.

Winchester, Simon. *The Map That Changed the World: William Smith and the Birth of Modern Geology.* New York: HarperCollins, 2001.

Zuravicky, Orli. *Map Math: Learning About Latitude and Longitude Using Coordinate Systems.* New York: PowerKids Press, 2005.

Online Resources

www.davidrumsey.com
The David Rumsey map collection. This online library contains around 20,000 historical and modern maps.

http://dma.jrc.it
The mapping collection of the European Commission Joint Research Center. Includes ineractive maps as well as maps documenting environmental and human disasters around the world.

http://etc.usf.edu/Maps/
The University of South Florida's online mapping library. The collection includes historical and modern maps from around the world.

www.lib.utexas.edu/maps
The University of Texas's online map library. The collection includes old CIA maps, historical maps, and thematic maps from around the world.

www2.lib.virginia.edu/exhibits/lewis_clark
An online exhibition at the University of Virginia with information on historic expeditions, including Lewis and Clark.

http://maps.google.com
Google's online mapping resource, includes conventional maps and satellite images for most of the world, as well as street-level photography of Western urban centers.

http://maps.nationalgeographic.com
National Geographic's online mapping service.

http://memory.loc.gov/ammem/gmdhtml/
Map collections from 1500–1999 at the Library of Congress. The collection includes maps made by early explorers, maps of military campaigns, and thematic maps on a variety of topics.

www.nationalatlas.gov
Online national atlas for the United States. Includes customizable topographic maps on a range of different themes.

http://strangemaps.wordpress.com
A frequently updated collection of unusual maps, from maps of imaginary lands to creative ways of displaying data in map form.

www.unc.edu/awmc/mapsforstudents.html
A large collection of free maps, covering many different subjects and regions, hosted by the University of North Carolina.

www.un.org/Depts/Cartographic/
english/htmain.htm
United Nations mapping agency website. contains maps of the world from 1945 to the present day, including UN maps of conflict areas and disputed territories.

Index

Page numbers written in **boldface** refer to pictures or captions.

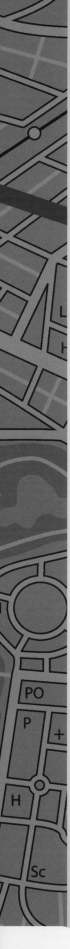